Cape Cod Cooking

The Cape Cod landscape offers many beautiful facets which include some of the most majestic sand dunes, long stretches of sandy beaches, salt marshes, ponds, bay streams, harbors, herring runs, productive farmlands and world famous cranberry bogs.

Oysters, mussels, fiddler and horseshoe crabs, quahogs, whelks, periwinkles, and razor clams live and reproduce in large numbers within our inlets and bays. Just off Cape Cod shores our waters are abundant with swordfish, squid, sharks, bluefish, striped bass, lobsters and the revered codfish.

Because of the relatively mild climate and favorable soil conditions, Cape Codders were highly productive farmers as well as fishermen and hunters. Native Americans shared their crops with early settlers. Squash, pumpkins, cranberries, wild blueberries, strawberries and apples were some of the regional fruits and vegetables. Corn was the staple food producing corn meal for porridge and bread.

Deer, duck, wild turkey and pigeon were among the game hunted by the early settlers. Pork and beef provided for boiled dinners while dairy cows and laying hens made it possible to produce eggs, cream and butter.

The Cape Cod flavor is sometimes spicy and sweet. Bacon and salt pork were used for frying while molasses, honey and maple syrup were used for sweetening. Rum, herbs and spices from seafaring captains from afar added flavor to the local cuisine.

Native Americans were the first to discover the fruits and game of the New World which is now evolved into the Cape Cod kitchen.

60 Favorite Recipes

Soups

Lobster Bisque

Melt butter and saute onion. Add flour to make roux, brown. Add lobster stock and tomato puree. Simmer until thickened. Remove from heat and add lobster meat.

Puree mixture in blender. Return mixture to pan and add light cream and milk; cook until throughly heated (not boiling) add nutmeg. Serves 4-6.

4 tablespoons butter
1 small onion, minced
2 tablespoons flour
1 pint lobster stock
2 tablespoons tomato puree
1 cup lobster meat
1 cup light cream
1 cup milk
pinch nutmeg

Cape Cod Clam Chowder

1 pint shucked clams, chopped,
   or two 6 ½ -ounce cans
   minced clams
2 ounces salt pork, diced, or 2
   slices bacon, cut up
2 medium potatoes,
   peeled and diced
1/2 cup chopped onion
2 1/2 cups milk
1 cup light cream
3 tablespoons all-purpose flour
1/2 teaspoon Worcestershire sauce

Drain clams, reserving liquid. Add enough water to reserved liquid to measure 2 cups; set aside. In a large saucepan fry salt pork or bacon till crisp; remove bits of pork or bacon and set aside. Add reserved liquid, potatoes, and onion to fat in saucepan. Cook, covered, about 15 minutes or till potatoes are tender. Stir in clams, 2 cups of the milk, and the light cream. Stir remaining 1/2 cup milk into flour; stir into chowder. Cook and stir till bubbly. Cook 1 minute more. Add Worcestershire, 3/4 teaspoon salt, and dash pepper. Sprinkle pork or bacon atop. Serves 6.

Portuguese Kale Soup

1 cup Kidney beans
1 large onion, chopped
1 pound chorico or linguica
1 pound Kale
1 tablespoon salt
1/2 teaspoon pepper
1 tablespoon vinegar
2 cups cubed potatoes

Soak beans overnight in cold water. In the morning, drain, add the onion, sausage (cut in pieces), kale (broken in pieces), salt and pepper and vinegar, and 10 cups water. Bring to boil, reduce heat and cook gently 2 to 3 hours. Add potatoes and 1 additional cup water. Continue cooking until potatoes are tender. Serves 6

Chatham Fish Chowder

In heavy soup pot fry bacon until crisp. Remove and set aside. In the hot fat fry onion until soft. Add the vegetable broth and 2 cups light cream, potatoes, seasoning and vinegar. Boil until potatoes are half done, add fish and continue cooking gently until fish is tender. Sprinkle bacon bits on top of each serving. Serves 6.

4 slices bacon
1 medium onion, chopped
2 cups light cream
2 cups vegetable broth
3 medium potatoes
1 teaspoon salt
1/4 teaspoon pepper
1/2 teaspoon saffron
1 tablespoon vinegar
2 pounds fish, (cod, flounder, haddock or halibut) cut into chunks

Cream of Mushroom Soup

In medium saucepan combine chicken broth, chopped onion, mushroom, and nutmeg. Bring mixture to a boil. Reduce heat, cover and simmer 5 minutes. Place mixture into blender container or food processor. Cover and blend for 30 to 60 seconds. Pour into bowl, set aside.

In same saucepan melt butter, stir in flour, salt and pepper. Add milk or half and half all at once.

Cook and stir until mixture is thick and bubbly.

Stir in the blended mushroom mixture. Cook and stir until thoroughly heated. Serves 4.

- 1 1/2 cup chicken broth
- 1/2 cup chopped onion
- 1 cup fresh mushroom, sliced
- 1/8 teaspoon ground nutmeg
- 2 tablespoons butter
- 2 tablespoons flour
- 1/4 teaspoon salt dash pepper
- 1 cup milk or half and half

Wellfleet Oyster Stew

In medium saucepan combine undrained oysters and salt. Cook over medium heat for 5 minutes or until edges of oyster curl. Stir in milk, cream and hot pepper sauce. Heat through. Sprinkle each serving with paprika and top with pat of butter. Serves 4.

- 1 Pint Shucked oysters
- 2 cups milk
- 1 cup light cream
- Dash hot pepper sauce
- Dash paprika
- 2 tablespoons butter
- 3/4 tablespoons Salt

Salads

Wilted Spinach Salad

Place spinach in large bowl, add the sliced green onion. Add pepper to greens. Cut uncooked bacon into small pieces. In large skillet cook bacon until crisp. Add wine vinegar to bacon and drippings, then stir in lemon juice, sugar and salt. Remove skillet from heat and add torn spinach and green onion. Toss until well coated. Top with chopped hard-cooked egg. Serve while warm. Serves 6.

8 cups fresh spinach - torn
1/4 cup sliced green onion
dash pepper
3 slices bacon
1 tablespoon white wine vinegar
2 1/2 tablespoons lemon juice
1/4 teaspoon sugar
1/4 teaspoon salt
1 hard-cooked egg, chopped

Lobster Salad Roll

2 cooked lobsters, about 1 1/2 lbs. each
2 tablespoons finely chopped onion
2 tablespoons finely chopped celery
1/2 teaspoon lemon juice
1/2 cup mayonnaise
4 soft rolls

Remove the lobster meat from tails and claws and chop into pieces. Combine lobster meat, lemon juice, onions, celery and mayonnaise. Fill soft rolls with mixture. Add lettuce if desired. Serves 4.

Cucumbers and Cream

3 medium cucumbers. sliced thin
1 medium onion, sliced thin
3/4 cup sour cream
1 1/2 tablespoons vinegar
1/2 teaspoon sugar
1/2 teaspoon salt

In large bowl combine cucumbers and onion. In separate bowl stir together sour cream, vinegar, sugar, and salt. Add mixture to cucumbers and onions, toss to mix thoroughly.
Cover and chill, stirring occasionally.
Makes 5 cups.

Tropical Fruit Salad

2 cups pineapple,
    cut into one inch chunks
2 cups canned or fresh mandarin
    orange slices
1 cup shredded coconut
1 cup tiny marshmallows
1 cup sour cream

In large bowl combine pineapple, mandarin oranges, coconut, marshmallows and sour cream. Cover and chill for several hours or overnight.

Layered Fruit Salad

1/4 cup walnuts, chopped
1 8 ounce package cream cheese
2 tablespoons lemon juice
1 teaspoon grated lemon peel
1/2 cup whipping cream
1/4 cup powdered sugar
2 cups blueberries
2 cups raspberries
2 cups strawberries, sliced
2 cups peaches, sliced

Combine cream cheese, lemon juice, and lemon peel, mix until well blended.
Beat whipping cream until soft peaks form, gradually add sugar, beating until stiff peaks form.
Fold whipped cream mixture into cream cheese mixture, chill. In 2 quart glass serving bowl layer peaches, blueberries, raspberries and strawberries.
Top with cream cheese mixture and sprinkle with nuts.
Chill. Serves 8.

Appetizers

Hot Crabmeat Dip
Chatham Fiesta Shrimp Cocktail
Lower Cape Clam Fritters
Shrimp Stuffed Mushrooms
Provincetown Stuffed Quahogs
Scallop and Bacon Skewers

Hot Crabmeat Dip

8 ounces cream cheese, softened
1 cup fresh crabmeat
2 tablespoons onion, finely chopped
2 tablespoons milk
1/2 teaspoon cream style horseradish
1/4 teaspoon salt, dash pepper
1/3 cup sliced almonds, toasted

Combine all ingredients except almonds, mixing well until blended. Spoon mixture into quiche pie plate, sprinkle with almonds. Bake at 375° for 15 minutes. Serve with crackers.

Chatham Fiesta Shrimp Cocktail

Toss all ingredients together in a medium glass or ceramic bowl and refrigerate for 60 minutes before serving. Serves 4.

1 pound medium shrimp, cooked, peeled and cleaned
3/4 cup italian salad dressing
1 medium tomato, diced
1 medium green chili, diced
1/3 cup green onions, sliced
2 tablespoons cilantro, chopped
2 teaspoons honey
1/4 teaspoon hot pepper sauce

Shrimp Stuffed Mushrooms

12 large mushrooms
6 large shrimp, cleaned and chopped into small chunks
1 onion, finely chopped
1 red pepper, finely chopped
2 cloves garlic, pressed
6 tablespoons butter
1/2 cup ritz crackers, crushed into fine crumbs
1/2 cup grated parmesan cheese

Remove stems from mushroom caps, set aside. Sauté caps in 2 tablespoons butter until just soft. Remove caps from pan and drain on paper towels. In same pan, add 2 more tablespoons butter and sauté mushroom stems (finely chopped), onion, red pepper, and garlic. Add the shrimp toward the end and cook until pink. Turn heat off and add ritz crackers and parmesan cheese, mix all ingredients well. Heat remaining butter and add enough to mixture to make moist. Fill mushroom caps with mixture and bake in 350° oven for 20 minutes. Serve with lemon wedges and hot sauce.

Lower Cape Clam Fritters

1 quart clams, finely chopped
1 cup flour
1 teaspoon baking powder
1 egg, beaten

Mix flour and baking powder together. Add the clams and egg. Drop tablespoonfuls into hot fat in deep skillet and fry until brown. Serves 6

Provincetown Stuffed Quahogs

12 large quahogs-save shells
1 pound mushrooms, chopped
1/2 cup finely chopped onion
1/2 cup melted butter
3 tablespoons butter for topping and frying
2 tablespoons flour
1 teaspoon salt
1/2 teaspoon black pepper
1 cup fresh bread crumbs,
hot sauce, lemon wedges .

Wash clams well to remove any grit and strain them in just enough water to cover. Remove clams and chop the meat. Sauté onions and mushrooms until they are soft. Blend in the flour and seasonings, stirring well. Add the chopped clams and stir, cooking until flour thickens. Set aside.

Mix bread crumbs with 1/2 cup melted butter. Butter the clam shells and fill with clam mixture. Top with bread crumbs, sprinkle with paprika and dot with butter. Bake in oven at 400 degrees for 10 minutes or until lightly browned. Serve with lemon wedges and hot sauce if desired.

Scallop and Bacon Skewers

1 1/2 pounds large sea scallops
   (20 scallops)
10 strips bacon
5 tablespoons butter, melted
1 lemon

Fry bacon until partially cooked. Drain on paper towel and cut each slice in half. Wrap bacon around scallop and thread onto metal or wooden skewer and brush with melted butter. Broil 6 inches from heat, turning occasionally and brushing with melted butter, until bacon is crisp and scallops are done (about 10 to 15 minutes). Serve with lemon wedges. Serves 4

Appetizer

Seafood

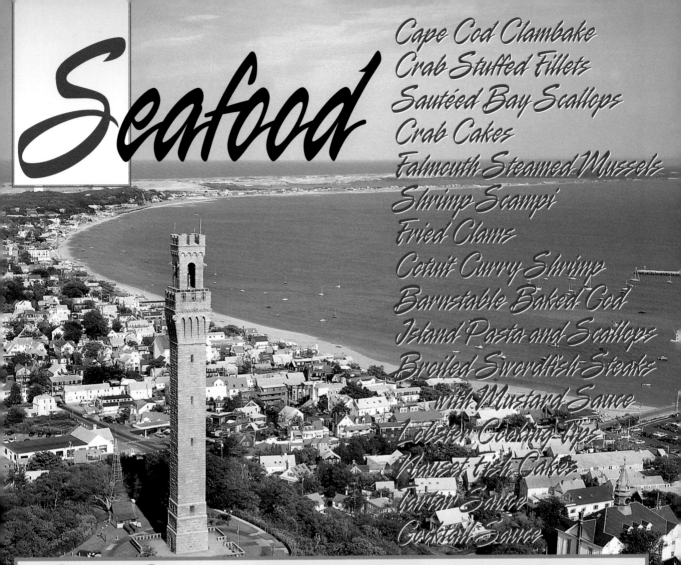

Cape Cod Clambake
Crab Stuffed Fillets
Sautéed Bay Scallops
Crab Cakes
Falmouth Steamed Mussels
Shrimp Scampi
Fried Clams
Cotuit Curry Shrimp
Barnstable Baked Cod
Island Pasta and Scallops
Broiled Swordfish Steaks
   with Mustard Sauce
Lobster Cooking Tips
Nauset Fish Cakes
Tartar Sauce
Cocktail Sauce

Cape Cod Clambake

4 dozen steamer clams
6 potatoes, skin on
6 ears corn, unhusked
6 whole medium onions
6 sausage
6 live lobsters, about 1 lb. each

Fill the botton of pot with 6 inches of wet seaweed. Divide the steamers among 6 pieces of cheesecloth and tie corners so you can pick them up. Place on seaweed. Remove silk and all but two layers of corn husk from corn. Place corn, potatoes, onions and sausage over the clams in that order. Top off with the lobsters. Put a layer of cheesecloth over the lobsters and cover with another 4 inches of seaweed. Cover loosely and place pot over high heat. When steaming begins, reduce heat to moderate and cook for one hour and 15 minutes.
Serve with hot crusty bread and melted butter.

Crab Stuffed Fillets

Preheat oven to 375°. Toss crabmeat with green pepper, onion, egg, mustard, worcestershire sauce and 1 tablespoon mayonnaise. Wash fillets and pat dry. Spoon egual amount of crab stuffing on fillets, roll and secure with toothpicks. Place in a greased baking dish. Spread a thin layer of mayonnaise on each fillet. Sprinkle with oregano and bake 20 minutes.

1 1/2 pound Cod or flounder fillets
1/2 pound crab meat
1/2 green pepper, chopped finely
1/2 onion, chopped finely
1 egg
1/2 teaspoon dry mustard
1/2 teaspoon worcestershire sauce
2 tablespoons mayonnaise
oregano

Sautéed Bay Scallops

In large skillet melt butter, add tarragon, shallots, and mushrooms cook until tender. Make a well in center of skillet and add scallops. Sauté both sides of scallops until opaque throughout (about 4 minutes). Pour wine over scallops and cook for 1 minute longer. Combine mixture adding parsley, serve with lemon wedges.

6 tablespoons butter
1/2 teaspoon tarragon leaves
3 tablespoons shallots, chopped
2 cups mushrooms, sliced
1 pound scallops
3 tablespoons dry white wine
1/2 cup chopped parsley

Crab Cakes

1 pound Crabmeat
1 egg slightly beaten
1/4 teaspoon dry mustard
1 1/2 teaspoon Worcestershire sauce
5 Ritz Crackers, crushed
1 Medium onion, minced
1 Green pepper, minced
2 tablespoons chopped parsley
1/2 teaspoon salt
1/4 teaspoon pepper

4 tablespoons vegetable oil

Mix together all ingredients except oil. Shape into patties. Saute in oil, over medium heat, a few minutes on each side until lightly browned.

Falmouth Steamed Mussels

4 tablespoons butter
1 onion, chopped
4 cloves garlic, minced, or pressed
1 cup dry white wine, or chicken broth
1/2 cup fresh parsley, chopped
3 quarts mussels, in shell, cleaned

In large kettle melt butter. Add onion and garlic, cook until soft. Add wine and parsley, bring mixture to a boil. Add mussels, cover and simmer gently until shells open (about 5 to 8 minutes). Discard any mussels that do not open. Serve with crusty bread for dipping into broth.

Shrimp Scampi

1/4 cup olive oil
1 pound shrimp, butterflied, in shell
1 stick butter
5 large cloves garlic, minced
2 tablespoons dry white wine
2 tablespoons parsley

Arrange shrimp shell side up on broiler rack. Brush with olive oil and lightly season with salt and pepper. Broil 4 minutes on side one and remove. Melt the butter in a skillet and cook garlic until tender, add wine and simmer for 2 minutes. Add the shrimp and parsley mix ingredients and cook for 2 more minutes. Garnish with lemon wedges. Serves 4

Fried Clams

2 cups clams, shucked
1/3 cup flour
1/2 teaspoon salt
1/8 teaspoon pepper
2 beaten eggs
3/4 cup fine dry bread crumbs
fat for deep frying

Drain clams and pat dry. Mix together flour, salt and pepper. Roll clams in flour mixture. Dip coated clams in mixture of beaten eggs and 2 tablespoons water, then roll in bread crumbs. Fry in hot fat until golden brown. Serve with tarter sauce and lemon wedges.

Cotuit Curry Shrimp

1 pound medium shrimp, peeled and cleaned
3 tablespoons butter
1 tablespoon olive oil
1 large onion
1 stalk celery
2 cloves garlic, minced
4 plum tomatoes, peeled and chopped
2 tablespoons hot curry powder

Sauté shrimp in butter and olive oil until pink (2 to 3 minutes). Remove shrimp from pan and add onion, celery, garlic and tomatoes, cook for 5 minutes. Add shrimp and curry powder mixing all ingredients together, cook for another 5 minutes. Serve over hot rice;

Barnstable Baked Cod

1 1/2 pounds fresh Cod Fish
1/4 pound butter
1 tablespoon lemon juice
1 tablespoon olive oil
1 1/2 cups soft bread crumbs

Preheat oven to 350°. Wash fish and pat dry. Melt butter, add lemon juice and olive oil. Spread mixture on fish and coat both sides with bread crumbs. Place in greased baking dish and bake for 20 minutes; Serves 4

Island Pasta and Scallops

12 ounces of small size pasta (shells or bows)
4 Tablespoons butter
8 ounces sliced mushrooms
4 ounces finely chopped bacon
1 cup sea scallops
4 ounces grated cheese

Cook pasta according to directions. In large skillet melt 3 tablespoons of butter. Add mushrooms and bacon. Sauté for 10 minutes and then add sea scallops. Cook for another 5 minutes. Remove from heat and serve over pasta that has been tossed with 1 tablespoon butter and grated cheese.

Broiled Swordfish Steaks with Mustard Sauce

3 swordfish steaks
4 tablespoons butter
1 tablespoons olive oil
1 tablespoons lemon juice
2 cloves garlic, minced
1 tablespoon parsley
1/2 teaspoon salt, dash pepper
1/2 cup mayonnaise
2 teaspoons mustard

Heat butter together with olive oil, lemon juice, garlic, parsley, salt and pepper. Baste fish well with mixture. Arrange on broiler pan and broil about 4 inches from heat until lightly browned for about 6 to 8 minutes. Turn fish and continue broiling until second side is lightly browned and fish flakes easily with fork. Mix together mayonnaise and mustard and spread on top of steaks. Then continue to broil until mustard sauce is lightly browned (watch closely). Serves 4

Lobster Cooking Tips

Boiled Lobster: Plunge a 1 or 1 1/2 lb. lobster into a large kettle of rapidly-boiling water. Cover tightly and cook for the suggested times listed. Serve with melted butter and lemon wedges.

For Steamed Lobster, plunge lobster into several inches of boiling water head first for a quick kill and let steam the suggested times listed.

1 LBS	12 minutes
2 LBS	18 minutes
3 LBS	22 minutes
4 LBS	25 minutes
6 LBS	32 minutes
8 LBS	35 minutes
10 LBS	40 minutes
15 LBS	44 minutes

Seafood

Nauset Fish Cakes

1/2 pound Cod or haddock
2 large potatoes, peeled
2 eggs, slightly beaten
1 large onion, diced
1 tablespoon flour
Fresh parsley, chopped
Salt and pepper to taste

Boil fish and potatoes together until cooked. Flake fish and mash potatoes. Mix fish, potatoes, eggs, onion, parsley and seasoning together well. Form the mixture into balls, flatten and dust with flour.
Fry in plenty of hot butter until browned. Traditionally served with baked beans. Serves 4.

Tartar Sauce

1 cup mayonnaise
2 tablespoons onions, chopped finely
2 tablespoons pickle, chopped finely
1 teaspoon lemon juice
1 tablespoon chopped parsley

Combine all ingredients and chill.

Cocktail Sauce

1 cup tomato ketchup
4 tablespoons horseradish
1/2 teaspoon hot sauce
1 teaspoon lemon juice

Combine all ingredients and chill.

Meats

New England Boiled Dinner
Roast Pork with Fennel Dijon
Beef Tenderloin Stroganoff
Roast Turkey with Harvest Stuffing
Dijon Chicken Breasts

New England Boiled Dinner

4-5 pounds corned brisket of beef
1 medium turnip, quartered
5 small parsnips, peeled and cut into chunks
6 small carrots, peeled
8 small onions, skinned
6 medium potatoes, peeled
1 medium cabbage,
    quartered and cored

Place beef in large heavy pot. Add enough water to cover meat. Boil gently for 3 to 4 hours until meat is almost tender. Add all ingredients. Cover and return to boil. Reduce heat and simmer for 15 to 20 minutes or until cabbage is soft.
Serves 6-8.

Roast Pork with Fennel

1 3 to 4 pound pork loin blade roast
1/2 teaspoon fennel seed
2 tablespoons sugar
1 teaspoon salt
1 teaspoon ground sage
1 teaspoon dried marjoram, crushed
1/4 teaspoon celery seed
1/4 teaspoon dry mustard
1 tablespoon snipped parsley

Stud roast with fennel seed inserting the tip of a knife into the meat and pushing 4 or 5 seeds into a meat pocket as you remove the knife. Cut about 15 evenly spaced pockets on meat's surface. Combine sugar, salt, sage, marjoram, celery seed, dry mustard, and 1/8 teaspoon pepper; rub roast with mixture. Cover roast; let stand 4 hours in refrigerator.
Place meat on a rack in a shallow roasting pan. Insert a meat thermometer. Roast, uncovered, in a 325° oven for 2 1/4 to 2 3/4 hours or till meat thermometer registers 170°. Place on a platter; sprinkle with parsley. Serves 8 to 10.

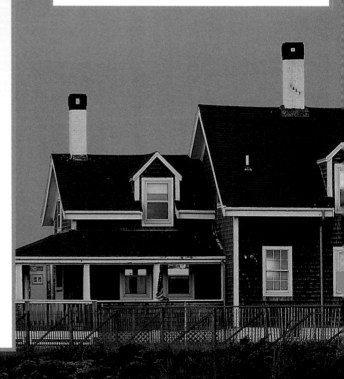

Beef Tenderloin Stroganoff

3 tablespoons vegetable oil
2 pounds tenderloin tips
1 medium onion, chopped
1/2 pound mushrooms
2 cloves garlic
1 cup white wine
1 cup sour cream
salt, pepper, cayenne

Cut tenderloin tips in 2 inch slices about 1/2 inch thick. Sauté with chopped onion over high heat in 2 tablespoons oil. Sauté mushrooms and garlic separatly in remaining oil. Combine two cooked mixtures and add all remaining ingredients. Simmer 5 minutes.

Roast Turkey with Harvest Stuffing

1 10-12 pound Turkey
1 Cup carrots, chopped
1 Cup celery, chopped
1/2 Cup onion, chopped
1/2 Cup butter
1/2 teaspoon ground Sage
1/2 teaspoon salt
1/8 teaspoon pepper
1/4 teaspoon ground cinnamon
8 cups dry bread cubes
2 cups apple, peeled, chopped
3/4 to 1 cup chicken broth

In skillet cook carrots, celery, and onion in butter till tender. Stir in sage, salt, pepper, and cinnamon. In a large bowl combine bread cubes and finely chopped apple. Add vegetable mixture and enough chicken broth to moisten. Lightly mix together. Loosely spoon stuffing into body cavity.

Brush skin of turkey with cooking oil and roast in uncovered pan at 325° for 4 to 5 hours.

Dijon Chicken Breasts

1/2 loaf country-style bread
1/2 cup freshly grated Parmesan cheese
1 tablespoon chopped fresh sage leaves
1 stick unsalted butter
4 tablespoons Dijon mustard
4 skinless boneless chicken breast halves

Preheat oven to 450° and line a baking sheet with foil. Tear bread into pieces and in a food processor pulse until finely ground. In a large bowl stir together 2 cups bread-crumbs, Parmesan and sage. Melt butter, add salt and pepper to taste. Pat chicken dry and brush all over with mustard mixture. Roll chicken in bread-crumb mixture, pressing gently to adhere and arrange chicken without crowding on baking sheet. Drizzle with butter. Bake chicken in middle of oven until cooked through and golden, 25 to 30 minutes.

Meats

Vegetables

Broccoli Casserole

1 pound fresh broccoli
1 can cream of mushroom soup
1 cup mayonnaise
1 3-ounce can french-fried onions

Cook broccoli until tender, drain. Combine mayonnaise and cream of mushroom soup. Lightly stir together broccoli, mayonnaise, soup mixture. Turn into 1-quart casserole dish and bake at 350° for 20 minutes. Then sprinkle french-fried onions and continue baking uncovered for about 10 minutes until onions are golden brown.

Parmesan Asparagus

1 pound fresh asparagus
1/4 cup olive oil
2 cloves garlic, minced
1/2 cup parmesan cheese, finely grated
2 teaspoons lemon juice

Steam asparagus for 8 to 10 minutes. Arrange steamed asparagus lengthwise in serving dish. Sauté garlic in olive oil, remove mixture from heat and add lemon juice. Lightly toss with asparagus and sprinkle with parmesan.

Cream Cheese Potatoes

1 1/2 pounds small red bliss potatoes, quartered
1 large red pepper, sliced
1 large onion, sliced
2 cloves garlic, minced
4 tablespoons butter, melted
1/2 teaspoon salt
8 ounces cream cheese, cubed

Preheat oven to 375°. In large bowl mix all ingredients except cream cheese. Arrange mixture in shallow 2 quart baking dish. Bake for 1 hour, stirring mixture once or twice. Add cubed cream cheese and continue baking for 20 minutes. Makes 4-6 servings.

"Highland" Mushroom Sauté

24 small or medium mushrooms
1 large onion chopped
3 tablespoons butter
2 cloves garlic, minced
1/3 cup dry red wine
2 tablespoons balsamic vinegar
1 tablespoon worcestershire sauce

Remove stem from mushrooms and clean caps. Sauté onions in butter until soft, add mushroom caps and continue sautéing until mushrooms and onions are golden brown. Add garlic and cook for 3 minutes. Add wine, vinegar, worcestershire, and cook until most liquid is absorbed.

Creamy Scalloped Potatoes

1 8-ounce package cream cheese
1 1/4 cup milk
1/4 teaspoon salt
1/8 teaspoon pepper
2 tablespoons chives, chopped
4 cups potatoes, sliced thin
dash paprika

Combine cream cheese, milk, salt and pepper. Cook over low heat until smooth, stirring frequently. Add potatoes and chives mixing lightly. Turn into 1 1/2 quart casserole dish. Bake covered for 45 minutes at 350° then uncover and continue to bake for another 30 minutes or till potatoes are done.

Cinnamon Squash

2 acorn squash
6 tablespoons butter, melted
1/2 teaspoon cinnamon
1 teaspoon brown sugar

Halve and seed squash. Place cut side down in shallow baking pan. Bake at 350° for 30 minutes. Turn cut side up and fill with mixture of melted butter, cinnamon and brown sugar. Bake 20 to 30 minutes longer.

Boston Baked Beans

3 cups navy beans
2 teaspoons salt
3 tablespoons molasses
2 tablespoons sugar
1/4 teaspoon mustard
1/2 pound salt pork

Soak beans overnight in cold water. Then bring to a simmer and cook until skins begin to burst. Drain. Put in a bean pot. Add salt, molasses, sugar and mustard mixed with 1 cup boiling water. Blanch the salt pork, scrape the surface of the rind and cut through every 1/2 inch. Bury it in the beans so that just the rind is exposed. Cover with boiling water and bake in a 300° oven. Add more water from time to time. Bury a small onion for extra flavor if desired. Bake 3 to 4 hours.

Breads and Muffins

Cranberry Apple Muffins
Banana Bread
Craigville Cranberry Bread
Brewster Cornbread
Blueberry Muffins

Cranberry Apple Muffins

Heat oven to 400°. Spray bottoms of 12 medium muffin cups with non-stick cooking sprays or line with paper baking cups. Beat milk, oil and egg whites in a large bowl. Stir in remaining ingredients except cranberries and apples just until flour is moistened (batter will be lumpy). Fold in cranberries and Apples. Divide batter evenly among muffin cups (cups will be full). Sprinkle with sugar if desired. Bake 20 to 25 minutes or until golden brown. Immediately remove from pan.

1 cup skim milk
1/4 cup vegetable oil
1 cup chopped peeled apples
2 egg whites or 1/4 cup cholesterol free egg product
1 cup all purpose flour
1 cup whole weat flour
1/3 cup sugar
3 teaspoons baking powder
1/2 teaspoon salt
1/4 cup fresh or frozen cranberries, chopped

Banana Bread

2 cups flour
1 teaspoon baking soda
1 teaspoon baking powder
1 teaspoon salt
2 eggs
1 cup sugar
4 very ripe bananas
1 teaspoon vanilla
1/2 cup vegetable oil
1 teaspoon cinnamon

Preheat oven to 350°. In a medium bowl combine flour, baking soda, baking powder and salt. In a large bowl cream together eggs and sugar. Stir in mashed bananas, vanilla, oil and cinnamon. Stir in flour mixture, a third at a time, until just combined. Divide batter into two 9x5 loaf pans. Bake for about 1 hour.

Craigville Cranberry Bread

2 cups flour
1 cup sugar
1 1/2 teaspoons baking powder
1/2 teaspoon baking soda
1 teaspoon salt
2 tablespoons shortening, melted
1 egg, well beaten
2 cups fresh cranberries, halved
Juice and grated rind of one orange

Sift together flour, sugar, baking powder, soda and salt. Combine orange juice, grated rind, melted shortening and enough water to make three-quarters cup of juice. Stir in beaten egg. Pour this mixture into the dry ingredients, mixing only enough to dampen. Fold in halved cranberries. Bake in greased loaf pan in moderate oven (350°) for 50 or 60 minutes.

Brewster Cornbread

1 cup all-purpose flour
1 cup yellow cornmeal
1/4 cup sugar
4 teaspoons baking powder
1/2 teaspoon salt
2 eggs
1 cup milk
1/4 cup cooking oil

Preheat oven to 400°. Stir together flour, cornmeal, sugar, baking powder and salt.
Add eggs, milk and oil.
Beat just until smooth. Put mixture into 9x9x2 inch baking pan.
Bake for 20 to 5 minutes.
8 or 9 servings.

Blueberry Muffins

1 cup fresh blueberries
1 3/4 Cup all-purpose flour
1/3 Cup sugar
2 teaspoons baking powder
1/2 teaspoon salt
1 beaten egg
3/4 cup milk
1/3 cup cooking oil
1 teaspoon finely shredded Lemon peel

Stir together all dry ingredients.
Combine egg, milk and oil. Add wet mixture all at once to dry ingredients. Stir just until moistened then fold in blueberries.
Bake in 400° oven for 20 to 25 minutes.
Makes 10 to 12 muffins.

Crumb Topping

1/4 cup light brown sugar
2 tablespoons flour
1 tablespoon butter

Combine ingredients and mix until crumbly. Sprinkle over muffins before cooking.

Desserts

Strawberry Shortcake
Apple Cranberry Pie
Indian Pudding
Sandy Neck Apple Pie
Boston Cream Pie
Hermit Cookies
Nobska Pecan Pie
Pumpkin Pie and
Pumpkin Bread

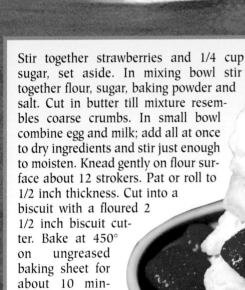

Strawberry Shortcake

Stir together strawberries and 1/4 cup sugar, set aside. In mixing bowl stir together flour, sugar, baking powder and salt. Cut in butter till mixture resembles coarse crumbs. In small bowl combine egg and milk; add all at once to dry ingredients and stir just enough to moisten. Knead gently on flour surface about 12 strokers. Pat or roll to 1/2 inch thickness. Cut into a biscuit with a floured 2 1/2 inch biscuit cutter. Bake at 450° on ungreased baking sheet for about 10 minutes until golden. Split and fill with fruit, add whipped cream, serve warm, serves 9.

6 cups fresh strawberries, slices
1/4 cup sugar
2 cup all purpose flour
2 tablespoons sugar
1 tablespoon baking powder
1/2 teaspoon salt
1/2 cup butter
1 egg, beaten
1/2 cup milk

Apple Cranberry Pie

1/2 cup sugar
2 tablespoons flour
1/4 teaspoon cinnamon
dash salt
1 teaspoon grated orange peel
1/2 cup maple syrup
1 tablespoon butter
1 1/2 cups cranberries
3 cups sliced peeled McIntosh apples
Pastry for 2 crust 9 inch pie.

Combine first 7 ingredients. Cook 2 minutes stirring until sugar dissolves. Add cranberries. Boil 2 minutes. Fold in apple slices and cool. Pour into pastry - lined 9 inch pan. Make lattice strips of pastry dough over filling. Trim edges. Bake at 425° for 40 - 45 minutes.

Indian Pudding

5 tablespoons cornmeal
1 guart milk
2 tablespoons butter
3/4 cup molasses
1 cup evaporated milk
1 teaspoon salt
3/4 teaspoon cinnamon
1/2 teaspoon ginger
2 well beaten eggs

Scald the milk with the cornmeal added; then mix in the butter, molasses, salt, spices and eggs. Pour into well-greased baking dish. Add evaporated milk but do not stir. Bake 1-hour at 350°. Serve warm with a scoop of ice cream.

Sandy Neck Apple Pie

6 cups tart apples, peeled and sliced
1 3/4 cups sugar
2 tablespoons flour
3 tablespoons butter
1 teaspoon cinnamon
1/8 teaspoon nutmeg
pastry for double crust pie

Combine sugar, flour, cinnamon, nutmeg, and apples.(For juicy pie omit flour) Toss to coat fruit. Pour into pastry lined 9 inch pie plate. Dot with butter. Adjust top crust. Seal and flute edge. Sprinkle top with sugar. Bake at 375° for about 30 minutes. Serves 8

Boston Cream Pie

Pie

1/2 cup butter
1 cup sugar
2 eggs beaten
2 cups flour, sifted
2 teaspoons baking powder
1/2 cup milk
1 1/2 teaspoons vanilla

Butter and lightly flour two 8-inch round cake pans. Preheat oven to 350°. Cream butter and sugar until light. Add eggs and mix well. Add dry ingredients alternately with milk. Add vanilla and spoon into cake pans. Bake for 30 minutes or until inserted toothpick comes out dry. Remove from pans when cool.

Cream Filling

1 cup milk
1/2 cup sugar
3 tablespoons flour
1/8 teaspoon salt
2 egg yolks
1 1/2 teaspoons vanilla

Heat milk in pan until very hot, then stir in sugar, flour, and salt. Cook over medium heat, stirring contantly until thick. Add egg yolks and cook continuing to stir for another 5 minutes. Remove from heat and add vanilla and cool stirring occasionally. Spread cream filling between cake layers when cooled.

Chocolate Frosting

2 one ounce squares unsweetened chocolate
3 tablespoons butter
1 cup powdered sugar
2 tablespoons hot water
1 teaspoon vanilla

Melt chocolate and butter over low heat, stir until smooth. Remove from heat and add remaining ingredients; mix well, spoon over top of pie letting it drip down sides.

Hermit Cookies

1/4 cup raisins or currants
1/4 cup chopped nuts
2 cups flour
4 tablespoons butter
1/2 cup sugar
1/2 tablespoon salt
2 eggs
1/2 cup molasses
1 tablespoon baking soda
1/2 tablespoon cream of tartar
1 tablespoon cinnamon
1/4 tablespoon mace
1/4 tablespoon nutmeg

Preheat the oven to 350°. Grease a 13-inch cake pan or some cookie sheets. Toss the raisins or currants and the chopped nuts in 1/4 cup of the flour; set aside. Cream the butter, then add the sugar and blend well. Add the salt, eggs, and molasses and beat well. Mix together the remaining 1 3/4 cups flour, the baking soda, cream of tartar, cinnamon, cloves, mace and nutmeg; add to the butter-sugar-egg mixture and beat thoroughly.
Stir in the raisins and nuts. Spread in the pan or drop by teaspoonfuls into the cookie sheets. Bake only until the top is firm and the center chewy, about 15-20 minutes for the squares or 8-10 minutes for the cookies.

Nobska Pecan Pie

1 cup pecan pieces	1/2 cup soft butter
2 tablespoons flour	dash of salt
1/2 cup sugar	1 cup light syrup
3 eggs	1 teaspoon vanilla
whipped cream	1 9-inch unbaked pie shell

Preheat oven to 375°. Mix flour together with sugar. Beat eggs slightly; add butter, salt, sugar mixture, syrup, nuts, and vanilla. Mix well and pour into unbaked pie shell. Bake for 10 minutes at 375° and then at 350° for 50 minutes more. Serve with whipped cream.

Dessert

Pumpkin Pie

1 1/2 cups cooked Pumpkin, mashed
1/2 teaspoon salt
1/2 teaspoon cinnamon
1/2 teaspoon ginger
1 1/2 cups evaporated milk
1/2 cup milk
2 eggs, slightly beaten
pastry for 9 - inch pie pan

Preheat oven to 425°. Line pan with pastry dough. Combine remaining ingredients in a large bowl and beat until smooth. Pour into lined pie pan and bake for about 45 minutes.

Pumpkin Bread

1 1/2 cups flour	2 eggs, beaten
1/2 teaspoon salt	1/4 cup water
1 cup sugar	1/4 teaspoon nutmeg
1 teaspoon baking soda	1/4 teaspoon cinnamon
1 cup pumpkin puree	1/4 teaspoon allspice
1/2 cup vegetable oil	1/2 cup chopped nuts

Preheat oven to 350°. Sift together flour, salt, sugar, and baking soda. Mix the pumpkin, oil, eggs, water, and spices together. Then combine with dry ingredients mixing just to moist, stir in the nuts. Pour into well greased loaf pan. Bake for 50 to 60 minutes until a toothpick comes out clean.

Jam and Jelly

Beach Plum Jelly
Plum Rum Jam
Strawberry Jam

Beach Plum Jelly

2 quarts beach plums
4 cups sugar

Cook beach plums in 2 1/2 cups water. Cook for about 25 minutes, mashing the plums carefully once or twice. Strain mixture through layers of cheesecloth. Do not squeeze the cloth or the jelly will become cloudy. Just leave it to drip slowly. Mix juice and sugar and bring to a boil and simmer for 10 to 30 minutes, or until the point of jelling is reached. Test by placing a small amount of the syrup in a spoon, cool it slightly, and let it drop back into the pan off the side of the spoon. If it falls into 2 drops, seperately, its not quite done. When jellied, these two drops should blend into one. Pour hot jelly into scalded glasses or jars and seal with pariffin wax.

Plum Rum Jam

3 1/2 cups plums, chopped fine
1/2 cup lemon juice
7 1/2 cups sugar
1 3/4 ounce package powdered fruit pectin
1/4 cup good dark rum

Combine plums, lemon juice, pectin, and sugar in kettle; boil hard for 3 minutes stirring constantly. Then add rum, stir at intervals for 5 minutes. Pour into jam jars and seal.

Strawberry Jam

8 cups strawberries, cleaned
1 3/4 ounce package powdered fruit pectin
2 tablespoons lemon juice
7 cups sugar

Crush strawberries and measure out 4 1/2 cups. In large kettle combine crushed berries, pectin, and lemon juice. Bring to a full boil, stir in sugar and return to a full boil. Boil hard, uncovered, for one minute, stirring constantly. Remove from heat and quicky skim off foam with metal spoon. Pour into jam jars and seal.